AT HOME with the GOPHER TORTOISE

THE STORY OF A KEYSTONE SPECIES

MADELEINE DUNPHY   Illustrated by Michael Rothman

Web of Life

CHILDREN'S BOOKS

*For Jennifer Welwood, who is at the center of the web of life
for so many people. With love and gratitude.*
—M.D.

*Dedicated to my wife Dorothy, my daughter Nyanza, Dorothy Schursky,
Marge Leffler, and Bud Leffler.*
—M.R.

*Special thanks to Joan Berish and Paul Moler for their invaluable scientific
expertise and for their dedication to the preservation of the gopher tortoise and
the other animals associated with it.*

The gopher tortoise lives in longleaf pine and scrub oak forests of the Southeastern United States. The areas shaded in yellow on this map show where the gopher tortoise lives.

Don't reach down that hole! You never know what you might find. There could be skunks, birds, frogs, snakes, or any number of other creatures. You might even find the animal that dug the hole—the gopher tortoise.

With its wrinkled, prehistoric-looking face and chocolate- brown patterned shell, the gopher tortoise is very important to many creatures. Why? Because more than 360 different kinds of animals live in its burrows!

The gopher tortoise digs burrows to survive, and in the process helps other animals. Burrows protect the tortoise and other creatures from the heat of the summer, the cold of the winter, and forest fires. Some animals use the burrow to find food; others use it as a safe haven to raise their babies. The gopher tortoise is called a "keystone" species because so many animals depend upon it for survival.

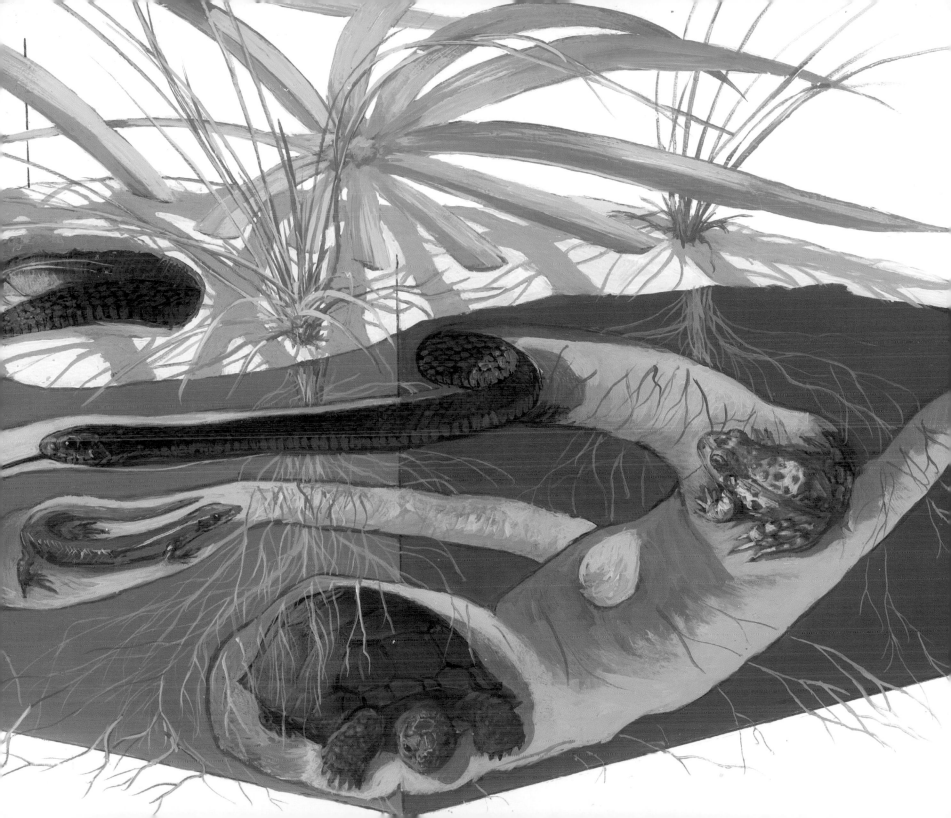

On a balmy night, the skunk uses the burrow for both shelter and hunting. The skunk eats mice, lizards, frogs, and other creatures. Since the burrow can be as long as a school bus, about 9 to 12 meters, some of these prey animals might even be in the same burrow as the skunk! They find hiding places in the tunnels and passages that twist around roots and rocks. But sometimes even a great hiding place isn't good enough.

One of the skunk's prey, the Florida mouse, digs a tunnel off the main route of the burrow. She builds a nest out of dried oak leaves, pine needles, and grass stems. With seeds, acorns, and nuts nearby to eat, this secret nest is an excellent place to raise her babies.

The burrowing owl is another animal that uses the burrow for nesting. Standing guard on its long, lanky legs, the male owl calls "hoo-hoo" near the entrance of the burrow.

Inside the burrow, the female incubates their eggs, while the male brings her food and protects their nest from predators.

Lots of buzzing and fluttering insects are drawn to the cool dampness of the burrow, and the gopher frog is one of the animals that hunts them. The frog squats at the entrance patiently waiting... Splat! The stocky black-spotted frog snares a bug with its lightning-fast tongue.

Some birds, such as
warblers, catch insects as
they fly out of the burrow
on sunny winter days.

From deep within the darkness comes the scuttling of whip scorpions...

...spiders

...crickets

...beetles

...and other creepy crawlers.

During the scorching summer and chilly winter, the indigo snake slides into the gopher tortoise burrow, where the temperature is comfortable. Slithering in and out of the burrow, this glistening, blue-black snake searches for small mammals, lizards, birds, frogs, toads, and other food.

On a sizzling summer day, a bobcat
nestles into the burrow to take
refuge from the blazing sun. The cool
temperatures inside make it a pleasant
place for a cat-nap. The bobcat curls into
a ball and snoozes until evening arrives.

A sparrow flees into
the burrow to escape a
ravenous red-tailed hawk.

Dappled feathered
bobwhites huddle
together inside to keep
warm on cold nights.

A lightning storm starts a
fire in the longleaf pine forest,
and animals run for their lives.
Smelling smoke, a rabbit zigzags
across the landscape and dives
into the safety of the burrow.

A lizard scurries
down the same
burrow as fire nears.

Even the burrow's front yard is important to some life-forms. The loose soil created by the tortoise's digging is perfect for growing plants, like the scrub mint, which fills the air with a refreshing scent.

The mole skink, a type of lizard, also likes this spot. It slithers through the sandy soil as it searches for something to eat.

This humble animal, the gopher tortoise, is at the center of the web of life for so many creatures. Although it may not know it, the tortoise builds homes for spiders, crickets, beetles, flies, frogs, snakes, mice, rabbits, birds, skunks, bobcats, and many others. A whole community of creatures depends upon the gopher tortoise, a keystone species, for survival.

MORE ABOUT THE
Gopher Tortoise

Gopher tortoises live in longleaf pine and scrub oak forests of the Southeastern United States. More than 360 different kinds of animals occupy gopher tortoise burrows, but not necessarily all at the same time. Some animals, like the burrowing owl, will only inhabit burrows that the tortoise has already abandoned, while others, like the Florida mouse, will live in burrows when the tortoise is present.

We know that many animals use the burrows, and that some of these, like the gopher cricket, live nowhere else in the world. If the gopher tortoise disappeared, what would happen to these animals? Many researchers fear that if this keystone species became extinct, many other species would soon follow.

Numerous threats face the gopher tortoise. The most significant threat is the loss of habitat due to new construction and agriculture. Another problem is the suppression of fire from the longleaf pine and scrub oak forests. Periodic natural fires play an important role in maintaining tortoise habitat by opening up the canopy and allowing sunlight to reach food plants below.

Even in the best conditions, the population of the gopher tortoise would still grow slowly because so many tortoise eggs and young fall prey to predators. Also, tortoises aren't able to reproduce until they are about ten years old.

The gopher tortoise is currently listed as a threatened species and is protected by law. The law protects only the gopher tortoise, but in so doing it also benefits the many creatures that depend upon gopher tortoise burrows for survival. To find out more, contact the Gopher Tortoise Council at www.gophertortoisecouncil.org.

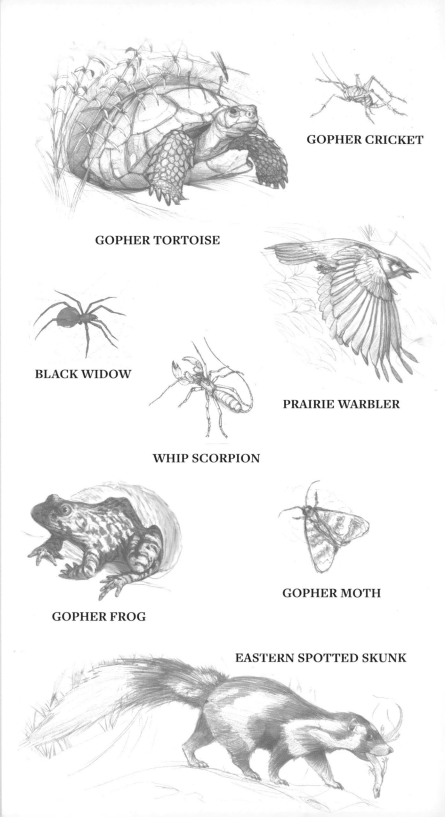

GOPHER CRICKET

GOPHER TORTOISE

BLACK WIDOW

PRAIRIE WARBLER

WHIP SCORPION

GOPHER MOTH

GOPHER FROG

EASTERN SPOTTED SKUNK